יַלְדָּה	תִּינוֹק	כֶּלֶב	חָתוּל
yaldah girl	*tinokk* baby	*kelev* dog	*chatool* cat

3

בְּגָדִים *bgadim* Clothes

סְוֶדֶר *svéder* jumper

תַּחְתּוֹנִים *tachtoenim* pants

נַעֲלַיִם *naalayim* shoes

4

גוּפִיָה
goofeeyah
vest

מִכְנָסַיִם
michnassayim
trousers

חֻלְצַת טְרִיקוֹ
***choo**ltzat **tree**ko*
t-shirt

גַּרְבַּיִם
*gar**bah**yim*
socks

5

אֲרוּחַת בֹּקֶר   *aroochat boker*   Breakfast

לֶחֶם
lechem   bread

חָלָב
chalav   milk

בֵּיצִים
beytzim   eggs

6

תַּפּוּחַ

tapooach   apple

תַּפּוּז

tapooz   orange

בָּנָנָה

banana   banana

הַמִּטְבָּח **ha-mitba**ch The kitchen

שֻׁלְחָן
*shoolcha*n table

כִּסֵּא
*kee**seh*** chair

צַלַּחַת
*tza**la**chat* plate

8

סַכִּין
sakin knife

מַזְלֵג
mazleg fork

כַּף
kaf spoon

סֵפֶל
sefel cup

צַעֲצוּעִים   tza'àtzooim   Toys

סוּס

soos   horse

כִּבְשָׂה

kivsah   sheep

פָּרָה

parah   cow

תַּרְנְגֹלֶת
tarnegolet hen

חֲזִיר
chazir pig

רַכֶּבֶת
rakevet train

קֻבִּיּוֹת
koobeeyot blocks

בִּקוּר **bee**koor A visit

סַבְתּוּש **sav**toosh Granny

סַבָּא׳לֶה **sa**baleh Grandpa

נַעֲלֵי בַּיִת naa**lay ba**yit slippers

12

מְעִיל

meheel   coat

שִׂמְלָה

simlah   dress

כּוֹבַע

kova   hat

הַפַּארְק ha-**pa**rk The park

עֵץ
etz tree

פֶּרַח
***peh**rach* flower

נַדְנֵדוֹת
*nad**neh**dot* swings

כַּדּוּר
***ka**dour* ball

14

מַגְלֵשָׁה מַגָּפַיִם צִפּוֹר סִירָה

maglehsha slide   *magafayim* boots   *tzipor* bird   *seerah* boat

הָרְחוֹב ha-ré**cho**v The street

מְכוֹנִית
meh**cho**nit car

אוֹפַנַּיִם
offa**na**yim bicycle

מָטוֹס
matos plane

מַשָּׂאִית
*masa*yit   truck

אוֹטוֹבּוּס
*o*toboos   bus

בַּיִת
*ba*yit   house

הַמְּסִבָּה *ha-messeebah* The party

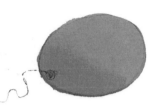

בָּלוֹן
balon balloon

עוּגָה
oogah cake

שָׁעוֹן
shaon clock

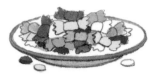

גְּלִידָה
*glee*dah ice cream

דָּג
dag fish

בִּיסְקְוִיטִים
biscvitim biscuits

סֻכָּרִיּוֹת
sookaryot sweets

19

בְּרֵכַת הַשְׂחִיָּה

*b**ré**chat ha-s**chi**yah*

זְרוֹעַ
*z**ro**wa*   arm

יַד
yad   hand

רֶגֶל
*r**é**gel*   leg

The swimming pool

כַּפּוֹת רַגְלַיִם
kapot raglayim
feet

בְּהוֹנוֹת
behonôt toes

רֹאשׁ
rosh head

יַשְׁבָן
yashvàn bottom

21

חֲדַר הַהַלְבָּשָׁה chadar ha-albashah

פֶּה
peh   mouth

עֵינַיִם
*ey**na**yim*   eyes

אָזְנַיִם
*oz**na**yim*   ears

The changing room

אַף
aff   nose

שֵׂעָר
seiar   hair

מַסְרֵק
masrek   comb

מִבְרֶשֶׁת
mivreshet   brush

23

הַחֲנוּת ha-cha**noo**t   The shop

אָדֹם
*á**do**m* red

כָּחֹל
*ka**cho**l* blue

יָרֹק
*ya**ro**k* green

24

צָהֹב
*tzaho*v yellow

וָרֹד
*varo*d pink

לָבָן
lavàn white

שָׁחֹר
*shahcho*r black

חֲדַר הָאַמְבַּטְיָה   cha**da**r ha-am**ba**tya

סַבּוֹן

*sa**bo**n*   soap

מַגֶּבֶת

*ma**gé**vet*   towel

שֵׁרוּתִים

*shéroo**ti**m*   toilet

The bathroom

אַמְבַּטְיָה

*am**ba**tya* bath

בֶּטֶן

***bé**ten* tummy

בַּרְוָז

*bar**va**z* duck

27

חֲדַר הַשֵּׁנָה   chadar ha-shénah   The bedroom

מִטָּה
*mee*tah   bed

מְנוֹרָה
ménora   lamp

חַלּוֹן
chalon   window

28

דֶּלֶת
delet door

סֵפֶר
sefer book

בֻּבָּה
booba doll

דֻּבִּי
doobee teddy

29

Match the words to the pictures

כֶּלֶב
kelev

מְנוֹרָה
mé**no**ra

דָּג
dag

גּוּפִיָּה
goofee**yah**

גְּלִידָה
g**lee**dah

כַּדּוּר
kadour

סְוֶדֶר
s**vé**der

רַכֶּבֶת
ra**ke**vet

מַזְלֵג
maz**leg**

בֵּיצָה
bey**tza**h

שֻׁלְחָן
shool**cha**n

סַכִּין
sa**ki**n

מַגָּפַיִם
maga**fa**yim

סֵפֶר
sefer

תַּפּוּז
ta**poo**z

פָּרָה	בֻּבָּה	כּוֹבַע	בַּרְוָז
*pa**rah***	***boo**ba*	*ko**va***	*bar**va**z*

חָלָב
*cha**lav***

עוּגָה
***oo**gah*

שָׁעוֹן
***sha**on*

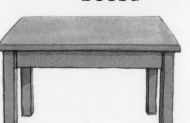

גַּרְבַּיִם
*gar**bah**yim*

בָּנָנָה
*ba**na**na*

דֻּבִּי
***doo**bee*

חַלּוֹן
*cha**lo**n*

מְכוֹנִית
*meh**cho**nit*

חֲזִיר	תַּפּוּחַ	חָתוּל	
*cha**zir***	*ta**poo**ach*	*cha**too**l*	

31

מִסְפָּרִים   *missparim*   Numbers

1 אַחַת
ahchat one

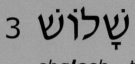

2 שְׁתַּיִם
shtayim two

3 שָׁלוֹשׁ
shalosh three

4 אַרְבַּע
arba four

5 חָמֵשׁ
chamesh five

1 אַחַת
ahchat one

2 שְׁתַּיִם
shtayim two

3 שָׁלוֹשׁ
shalosh three

4 אַרְבַּע
arba four

5 חָמֵשׁ
chamesh five

Hebrew alphabet

Here are the letters in the Hebrew alphabet. There are no capital letters in Hebrew, but five letters have different forms when they appear at the end of a word.

Name of letter	Hebrew letter		Sound	Pronunciation
alef	א		a	as in apple
bet	בּ		b	as in bed
vet	ב		v	as in wave
gimmel	ג		g	as in girl
jimmel	ג׳		j	as in jet
dalet	ד		d	as in dog
hey	ה		h	as in hat
vav	ו		v	as in vase
zayin	ז		z	as in zoo
chet	ח		ch	as in loch
tet	ט		t	as in tree
yod	י		y	as in yellow
kaf	כּ		k	as in king
chaf	כ	final form: ך	ch	as in loch, but with a stronger, more throaty sound than chet
lamed	ל		l	as in leg
mem	מ	final form: ם	m	as in mat
nun	נ	final form: ן	n	as in number
samech	ס		s	as in sun
ayin	ע		a	as in apple, but a more throaty sound than alef
pey	פּ		p	as in pen
fey	פ	final form: ף	f	as in safe
tzadi	צ	final form: ץ	tz	as in cats
kof	ק		k	as in king, but a stronger sound than kaf
resh	ר		r	as in red
shin	שׁ		sh	as in ship
sin	שׂ		s	as in sun
taf	ת		t	as in tree

Vowels

In Hebrew, the vowel sounds (e.g. "a" or "u") are shown by dots and lines under, above or next to the letter. These are only used in books for children and beginners, and in poetry and prayer books. They are not normally used in handwriting. In the examples below, the vowel marks are shown with the letter ט tet.

Name of vowel mark	Mark	Sound	Pronunciation
kamatz	טָ		
patach	טַ	ta	as in tar
chataf patach	טֲ		
segol	טֶ		
chataf segol	טֱ	te	as in ten
tzerei	טֵ		
chiriq	טִ	tee	as in tee
cholam male	טוֹ		
cholam chaser	טֹ	to	as in torch
kamatz qatan	טָ		
chataf kamatz	טֳ		
shuruq	טוּ		
kubutz	טֻ	too	as in too
shwa	טְ	te (silent)	

Note: In this book, a break in a word is shown by the ' sign.

Word list

This list shows all the words in this book in the alphabetical order of the English words. Next are the Hebrew words written in Hebrew letters, then a guide to show you how to say it. Remember, Hebrew is read from right to left.

English	Hebrew	Pronunciation
apple	תַּפּוּחַ	ta**poo**ach
arm	זְרוֹעַ	z**ro**wa
baby	תִּינוֹק	**ti**nokk
ball	כַּדּוּר	**ka**dour
balloon	בָּלוֹן	ba**lon**
banana	בָּנָנָה	ba**na**na
bath	אַמְבַּטְיָה	am**ba**tya
bathroom	חֲדַר אַמְבַּטְיָה	cha**dar** am**ba**tya
bed	מִטָּה	**mee**tah
bedroom	חֲדַר שֵׁנָה	cha**dar shé**nah
bicycle	אוֹפַנַּיִם	offa**na**yim
bird	צִפּוֹר	tzi**por**
biscuits	בִּיסְקְוִיטִים	bisc**vi**tim
black	שָׁחֹר	shah**cho**r
blocks	קֻבִּיּוֹת	koobee**yo**t
blue	כָּחֹל	ka**cho**l
boat	סִירָה	see**ra**h
book	סֵפֶר	**se**fer
boots	מַגָּפַיִם	maga**fa**yim
bottom	יַשְׁבָן	yash**vàn**
boy	יֶלֶד	**ye**led
bread	לֶחֶם	**le**chem
breakfast	אֲרוּחַת בֹּקֶר	aroo**chat bo**ker
brush	מִבְרֶשֶׁת	miv**re**shet
bus	אוֹטוֹבּוּס	**o**toboos
cake	עוּגָה	**oo**gah
car	מְכוֹנִית	meh**cho**nit
cat	חָתוּל	cha**too**l
chair	כִּסֵּא	kee**seh**
changing room	חֲדַר הַלְבָּשָׁה	cha**dar** alba**shah**
clock	שָׁעוֹן	**sha**on
clothes	בְּגָדִים	bga**dim**
coat	מְעִיל	meh**ee**l
comb	מַסְרֵק	mas**rek**
cow	פָּרָה	pa**rah**
cup	סֵפֶל	**se**fel
Daddy	אַבָּא'לֶה	**ah**bahleh
dog	כֶּלֶב	**ke**lev
doll	בֻּבָּה	**boo**ba
door	דֶּלֶת	**de**let
dress	שִׂמְלָה	sim**lah**
duck	בַּרְוָז	bar**va**z
ears	אָזְנַיִם	oz**na**yim
egg	בֵּיצָה	bey**tza**h
eggs	בֵּיצִים	bey**tzim**
eyes	עֵינַיִם	ey**na**yim
feet	כַּפּוֹת רַגְלַיִם	ka**pot** rag**la**yim
fish	דָּג	dag
five	חָמֵשׁ	cha**me**sh
flower	פֶּרַח	**peh**rach
fork	מַזְלֵג	maz**leg**
four	אַרְבַּע	**a**rba
girl	יַלְדָּה	yal**dah**
Grandpa	סַבָּא'לֶה	**sa**baleh
Granny	סַבְתּוּשׁ	**sav**toosh
green	יָרֹק	ya**ro**k
hair	שֵׂעָר	sei**ar**

First hundred words in Hebrew

Heather Amery

Illustrated by Stephen Cartwright

Translation and pronunciation guide by
Quarto Translations

Designed by Mike Olley and Jan McCafferty

 There i̶̶̶̶̶̶ every picture.

הַסָּלוֹן   *ha-sàlon*   The living room

אַבָּא׳לֶה
***ah**bahleh*   Daddy

אִמָּא׳לֶה
***ee**maleh*   Mummy

יֶלֶד
***ye**led*   boy

2